NOW IS TOO SOON

By Star L. Courtney

Fleming H. Revell Company
Old Tappan, New Jersey

Library of Congress Cataloging in Publication Data

Courtney, Star L
  Now is too soon.

    1. Mothers—Prayer-books and devotions—English.
    2. Parent and child. I. Title.
BV283.M7C68   242′.8   73-22358
ISBN 0-8007-0652-8

A
Mother's
Prayers
As
Her
Daughter
Nears
Marriage

The Day
After Christmas

Dear God, tonight there is disquiet in my heart. My eighteen-year-old daughter, a college freshman home for the holiday that marks Your birth, has a date with a young man new to her father and me.

Yes, he is a man and not a boy. This is the seed of my concern. In many ways she is a child yet.

I pray for Your loving watchfulness. Take care of her.

I am perplexed, Lord, that she has broken a previous date in order to go out again with last night's young man. Such fickleness is not in character. She shrugs off the other boy's disappointment as though she is helpless against Fate.

Dear Jesus, why do I panic? An escort attentive to her is nothing new! Enamored boys have crossed our threshold since her fourteenth birthday. She is an informed girl with Christian ethics, a girl levelheaded beyond her years. She can cope—I think—with the temptations that have lured others to destruction.

Then why am I alarmed, Lord?

I am reporting in, God. . . .

For the third night in a row the young man was here, saying the proper words to her father and to me, wearing the proper clothes (not grubs as the younger boys do), making a proper impression. Instead of rejoicing at the improvement in her choice of companion, I am terrified. He is twenty-two: he is too old—*too old!*

The dagger of premonition twists deeper when I observe how handsome they are together, she with peach skin and long, fine hair the color of sunshine— he so strikingly dark. Even in a crowd they will attract attention for their bodies are large-framed and tall, larger and taller than most, without being freaky. They radiate superb health and vital energy.

Yes, they are well-matched.

But we don't want a match for her! Not yet. She has completed only one-eighth of her college education. Ahead—before marriage—are many more young men to meet, many experiences to savor. Knowing others will help her to know herself.

We want, for her, the wisdom that comes with maturity before she chooses a lifetime mate. Too, we want her to have fun before she settles down.

Are these wicked desires, Lord? Is this selfishness on the parents' part?

We think not.

It is afternoon, and he is here. Why has he not waited until darkness for a traditional date? Why do my daughter's eyes shine?

Dear God, truly I am grateful that they are content to spend time together in this household where privacy is found mainly in the dictionary.

Then why am I so nervous?

He ate dinner with us tonight, and my daughter was radiant. Precious Saviour, how can I insulate her from pain? A romance so premature must end.

Don't forget, Lord, she is only eighteen!

My Lord and Master, I am calm now, touched by Your steadying hand. Thank You. Through Your influence I have switched my attitude from fear to confidence. Now I can concentrate on that which is positive: the growing maturity of my daughter.

For the first time since embracing college life with its freedom from parental rule, she is home for longer than a brief overnight. Her father and I see signs that she is judging us with new compassion—new approval. The parent-daughter wars are behind us—hopefully.

In all sincerity I thank You, God, that she is having a joyous and memorable holiday. I can accept without jealousy the fact that neither her father nor I is responsible for her current happiness. We remember how it was . . . ! Oh, how we remember!

He is a decent boy—we think—a worthwhile boy. A boy with a Christian upbringing. He is, in fact, the kind of boy we want her to marry.

But later, Lord. *Later!*

Good Shepherd, how we need You now! Please protect the eighty-mile stretch of highway down which my daughter and her young man travel. For them, lift the billows of blinding fog. Melt the patches of ice. Grant skill to oncoming drivers who—with too much alcohol—"Ring out the old; ring in the new."

Too, ease the torture in my heart. Did I do right? Did I do wrong? At what stage must a parent quit ordering, "Absolutely not!"? For that is what I longed to do—veto an out-of-town party on this most dangerous of nights.

She knows we preferred that she stay home, but the allure of the big-city party was too great. So guard her, God. Guard her and guide her.

Temptations are inherent in this night. Help her to resist them. Help her remember that legally and morally, she must not taste liquor. If he drinks (and I suppose he does, dear God) grant him the wisdom of moderation. Give him moral stamina to silence the coaxings that will tremble to his lips, for he is a mature man with a mature man's lusts and needs, and she is an affectionate girl. Don't let her forget in one night a lifetime of moral instruction.

Yes, Good Shepherd, please stay with her, and with him to whom we entrust her self-respect, her reputation—and in his car, her very life.

She has returned safely. Thank You, God!

New Year's Day, Noon

He is here again, and she is frying eggs for him. How can she fake such a domestic act, considering her lifelong reluctance to master the household arts?

Not that he would notice if she cooked the eggs in chocolate sauce! Both of them are dazed to the realities around them. They see only each other.

King of Kings! Lord of Lords! If this is the giant passion—the permanent love of their lives—please postpone its culmination for years and years. She is eighteen. *Only eighteen!*

Now is too soon.

Master, my husband has buried his head in the sand. When pressed, he mentions, "Ships that pass in the night."

Sweet Jesus, it is true that our daughter is the veteran of flirtations which—like flash floods and flash fires—come and go, the danger quickly past. But this time the signs are different.

My Comforter and Consoler, do not allow me to build a mountain out of a molehill. Remind me that ships indeed do pass in the night; and in the morning, there is no mark where they have been.

"This too shall pass," says Your Book.

13

Infinite Spirit, *listen* to me! In our lexicon, long-stemmed red roses are a declaration of love. The dozen roses that arrived today are so tall that to contain them, the florist fashioned one extra-long box from two.

What beauty in the sight and scent of these blooms! What a preview of Heaven You have provided here on earth!

Yet my enjoyment is marred. I fear this bouquet is a serious symbol. I fear the pattern of our lives is challenged.

Father, may these flowers be merely the tender dog biscuits of puppy love. May they mark only a fleeting infatuation!

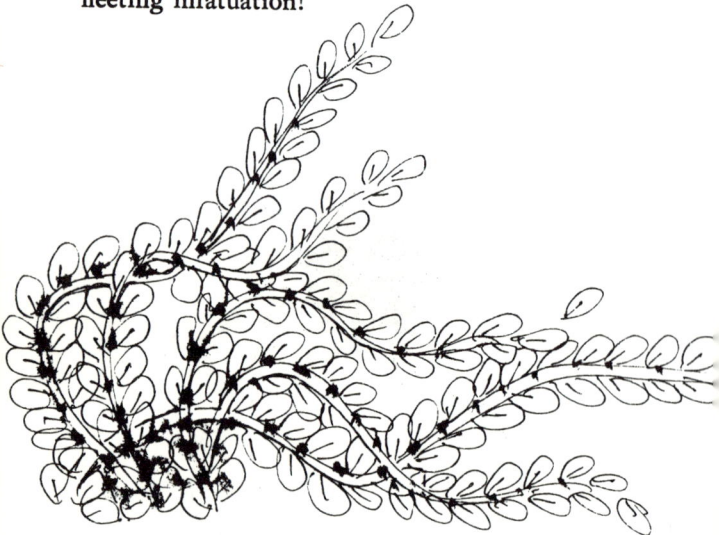

I notice that my daughter is hoarding other souvenirs of this romance—small gifts and sentimental trinkets—even a frosted gingerbread man off somebody's Christmas tree. How I remember doing the same!

Jesus, I admit a twinge of regret for youth that is past. Please insulate me from the sin of jealousy.

My Father, the time is fast approaching when they must separate, each returning to a college campus. If my gladness is a sin, please forgive me.

"Out of sight—out of mind," I tell myself, and a haunting voice replies, "Absence makes the heart grow fonder." A clear case, Lord, of the lady or the tiger.

They are together constantly now, on a merry-go-round of visits, introducing each other to old friends. It seems as if they are trying desperately to mesh their two worlds. Truly their worlds have been separate to this point despite their growing up in a common community and in the very same church. Four years! How vast is this age gap during childhood. How small—later.

Between eighteen and twenty-two, there still remains a chasm. Dear Lord, give me the wisdom to instruct and not anger my daughter when I point out this fact.

Have you noticed, Lord, that romance has its humor? Today the young man is driving my daughter back to her campus en route to his. *En route!* Not even the most perplexed map reader could see correlation between the two destinations. This has to be a detour to end all detours.

When he arrived today, his shirts and jackets and dress pants were hung on one-half of a rod suspended from the hanger-hooks of his car, his jeans in neat piles on one-half of the back seat. The other half was clearly reserved for my daughter's belongings, a his/hers arrangement that pierced my heart. Oh, how matter-of-factly the two of them loaded her clothes beside his!

Next to his single suitcase in the trunk went her multiple ones—her hair drier, her makeup mirror, her wig case—all the female paraphernalia. If he was amused by the quantity or nature of her posessions, he gave no sign.

They departed. It was an "into the sunset" finale, symbolic of an ending combined with a new beginning.

My emotions are strangling me. Saviour, please do not let me turn into a nervous mother at this late stage—not when my child-rearing task is nearly complete. *Nearly* complete . . . !

Is that, Lord, what is bothering me?

King of Heaven, what I need now is the wisdom
and strength to help my husband. Having been dis-
placed, he is suffering. Apparently to him the ordeal
of returning her to college—bag and baggage—is
not an ordeal at all but rather a labor of love! It
symbolizes, I suppose, one last bit of service and
homage to Her Majesty, an only daughter.

He has been her willing slave for eighteen years.
Of course it pains him to be superseded.

Even so, he fails to see this young man as a threat
to her carefully planned future. Perhaps he is pur-
posely blind.

I have weapons, Lord. I can comfort him with my
body and with my words.

Help me to act with understanding and compassion.

A new month. I pause for inventory.

All-Powerful God, we are pleased that our daughter remains a frequent letter writer. What a relief to learn she is dating on her own campus, not brooding about separation from her holiday suitor.

But the complexion of her letters has changed, Lord. They are more thoughtful—more sober. The tanglements of life are coming under her scrutiny, and she is groping for answers. She is, I suppose, maturing.

She does mention the hometown young man. He phones. He writes. She is not giddy; she is not wallowing in puppy love. (Perhaps the romance is blowing over?)

These are crucial days for her, Saviour. Stay with her.

Understanding Master, my husband and I have a problem. What can we do? Our daughter has asked permission to visit the young man on his campus where there are weekend-long festivities in observance of Saint Valentine's Day.

"Sweethearts should be together on Valentine's Day," she informed us.

Oh, God, she is too inexperienced to face the temptations of such a weekend. She is to unseasoned for him.

We registered our reluctance, Lord; in the same breath—we granted permission. Chalk up a victory for Human Nature. We know our daughter's limitations. She is obedient as long as our demands are reasonable in her eyes. When she phoned she supplied the answers before we asked questions: where she would sleep and the complete weekend agenda.

Creator, in Your wisdom You must guess what frightens us. If we once say *no,* will she launch a secret life? We do not want her off campus without our knowledge. Yet that would be so simple. In line with new collegiate freedom, her dormitory sets no residence restrictions—maintains no hours. The note-from-parents-to-housemother requirement is obsolete.

This is Your world, God. Why are You letting it change so fast? Help us to cope!

Sweet Jesus, our daughter has made a commitment to the young man. But *what* commitment? Even she does not seem to know.

This we do know. Proudly she is wearing his crested jewelry, warning all others: KEEP AWAY. THIS GIRL IS TAKEN.

How foolish! At eighteen, she has many, many more young men to meet and date—many, many more viewpoints to hear and judge. She still needs mental elbowroom to test herself. Why, she cannot even settle on a college major—a blueprint for her working life. How then can she dare to blueprint her emotional life?

She is so certain of herself! And of him! But Lord, bits and pieces of information are not the same as knowledge, are they? Knowledge comes from the sifting of experience. Today she is barely acquainted with herself.

Our Father, please slow her pace. Grant her all the ingredients of a full life—each in its own time.

Haunted by her new relationship with the young man, I lay sleepless last night and I am ineffective in my tasks today. Lord of Lords, we read so much nowadays about The New Morality. Am I out-of-date to consider this peculiar term a synonym for Old-Fashioned Immorality? How does all this sleep-together propaganda color the modern boy-girl relationship? What demands will the young man make on my daughter?

Jesus, help me concentrate on her levelheadedness. She is not a pushover—of that I am sure. She is, however, a creature of today's society.

With a backlog of instruction and advice, she is on record as a believer in chastity. But she is human! In the emotional vacuum before one falls in love, moral pledges are simple to make. Face-to-face with the reality of decision, such pledges are not easy to honor.

For moral strength, guide her to You, Saviour.

Our attitude toward the young man is changed. He is a magnet drawing her away from us—and we are angry.

Now she is telling us she will not finish college. Her degree is too distant—she is only in her second of eight semesters. The oncoming years are too precious to fritter away in classes, she claims. The achievement of a diploma is meaningless.

There are many arguments to support our position and so we reason with her.

But stubbornness is incompatible with reason, and she is stubborn. So are we.

Mend this break, Wise Jesus.

God, now I have doubts about doubting! My daughter and her young man are home, of course, on Easter break. It is uncanny how already they are a unit, not merely two individuals. Already their dialogue is tinted with private nuances meaningful to them.

My Saviour, I feel shut out!

Her life is still in my care and so I had to mention sex and its pitfalls.

Now she is angry with me—and insulted.

King of Glory, when should a mother's instruction end? Guide me, please, as I guide her.

Direct my treacherous tongue.

They are beautiful in church together, God—one bowed head so blonde, one so dark.

Forgive my maternal snoopiness, Redeemer. I cannot help wondering what looms ahead for them. A lifetime of Easter mornings at worship together? or is today merely a jelly bean in the basket that is my daughter's life—a sweet soon to be lost or abandoned in the cellophane grass that is Experience?

Please clue me in, Holy Friend!

26

People are telling me that young marriages have merit. Is the handwriting so bold against the wall?

My Comforter, of course I know that a wholesome young man is a buffer against the temptations of the drug scene and promiscuous sex. How warped our society, that this is a consideration!

Show us how to patch our frayed world, dear God. Guide us on our return route to Eden.

This is a strange summer, God, with the young couple separated by distance and—increasingly lately—by differences in opinion. They are making each other miserable.

He is on his campus, earning his final credits toward graduation. She is developing muscles in her right shoulder and arm, scooping bulk ice-cream into cones for barefoot children. It is a job of small glamour and negligible romance.

She is moody and troubled.

Be with her, Lord, as she examines and reexamines her relationship with the young man.

Help her to judge clearly.

The crested jewelry has been returned to the young man, and my daughter acts as though she has recovered from a long illness.

For breaking this unsuitable romance without shattering her heart, I thank You, God.

For silencing my lips when I started to say, "I told you so!" I *doubly* thank You.

Young men are here night and day, and they delight us by their abundance. Our daughter's social life is crammed. How much she missed by going steady! We rejoice that phase is over.

As the summer wanes, she throws herself into a headlong quest for fun. Often she is the instigator of parties. She laughs. She chatters. She teases.

But there is indication her good spirits is a surface thing—a coat of armor. Happiness does not glisten in her eyes as before. She tenses whenever the telephone rings.

Is she asking You for strength, God? Help her to turn to You in her confusion—today and every day of her life.

There has been a reconciliation—my daughter is ecstatic.

What *now*, Lord?

We trust You to guide us all.

Almighty Sovereign, there is rebellion in our ranks. Faced with separation from the young man, our daughter refused to return to her college campus. It is not education she is resisting, she said. If we are hung up on the idea of her continuing classes, she will enroll in the college nearest his job.

This she granted grandly, with the narrow and selfish generosity of the young.

In our viewpoint, education is an opportunity. To her, it is an ordeal. Yet she is gifted scholastically.

Why can't she view the future in long-range terms, Wise Leader?

The offer to attend school near his job is a red herring. He has no job as yet—nor do his prospects loom bright.

We have agreed to a compromise. Our daughter will earn credits by correspondence, meanwhile continuing work at the ice-cream shop. This combination should pall by semester's end. By next semester she should be back on campus.

King of Glory, watch over her!

Formally—on the verge of melodrama—the young man asked for our daughter's hand in marriage. His was a sober presentation of his assets (and not without charm).

Oh, but how skimpy are his assets! His recently conferred bachelor's degree (from a second-rate college) is in an overcrowded field. The mediocrity of his grades indicates he will not be among the first chosen for vacancies that might occur.

To his credit, he has not been lax in pursuing employment. He speaks of resumés, of interviews, of tests endured.

He harbors no suspicion that the work force might be saturated—that there is no job waiting for him. He is relaxed and patient, fully expecting "the right contact" or "the right coincidence" to provide employment.

This cocky attitude irks me, Lord. Too vividly do I recall the Great Depression. Holy Comforter, remind me that his only contact with Hard Times was on the pages of a textbook. No wonder he does not fear poverty, joblessness, hunger . . . !

But these conditions exist!

Holy Father, guide my speech as I struggle to explain economic facts to these youngsters who wallow so comfortably in self-confidence.

Our daughter dictated our answer to the young man's formal question.

"Yes," we agreed.

But our affirmation has strings attached. *No job— no marriage!*

This is reasonable—is it not, Lord?

Dear Deity, I am suffering doubts. The more I see of her young man—the more I panic. He is not good enough for her. He is not! *He is not!*

Right now she trails him in maturity. What will happen in a few years when she outgrows him mentally? By all tests and rankings, her potential is tremendous. She needs the stimulation of an equally gifted mind.

At this point, the man of her choice cannot even support her. He remains unemployed.

We see in him restlessness and irritability. Does he have the strength of character to remain a faithful and Christian husband? Or, through his weakness, will he break her heart?

God, please open her eyes to his flaws as well as to his charms.

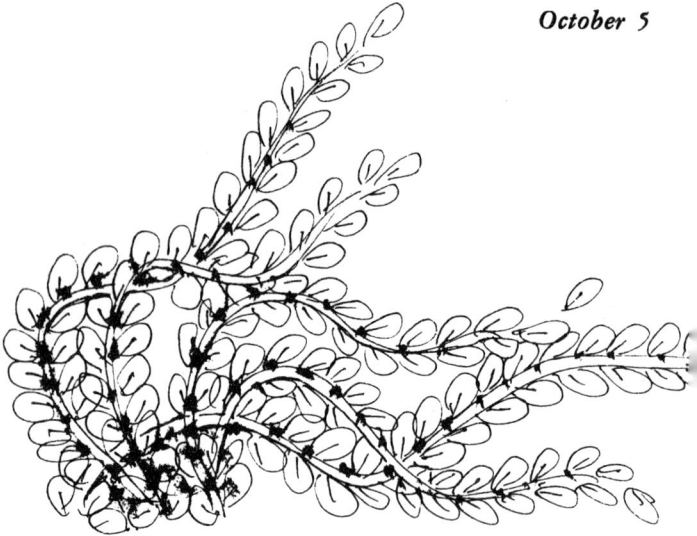

Master, I look back one page and suffer embarrassment.

Please understand that our opposition to this match is not weighted one-sided against the young man. Flaws exist is our child, too. She is fanatically stubborn. Her temper is quick, hot, and knife-edged. Time and experience will dull these unpleasant traits.

Meanwhile, should she not postpone marriage—life's most intimate and most difficult relationship?

Filter wisdom into her awareness, Father.

There is no momentum to the young man's job-hunting endeavors. Every lead has fizzled. He is freeloading on his parents when he should be supporting himself.

Brace yourself, Almighty. Today he announced disinterest in business. Suddenly he yearns to do something "meaningful." (Gainful employment is not "meaningful," apparently!)

Sweet Saviour, walk with me till I control my bitterness. Let me not think what-might-have-been. Help me concentrate on the strengths of this young man and not on his weaknesses.

Help me to build faith in his future.

Redeemer, there is a deterioration in the relationship between my daughter and me at the time it should be closest. How defensive she is! She snarls at any query about their future.

But how can I seal my lips, Lord? Newlyweds cannot live in a vacuum. They must arrange housing. There must be a source of income.

I read with gnawing in my stomach about communes and a new group pattern for living. Is such a settlement their destination?

I would find strength to accept that, I think, oh, Jesus. What I cannot accept is their total unconcern for the obligations of the future.

Lord, I will never understand the Now generation. When I beg You, "Bring us closer together," my plea actually is, "Shift their values nearer to ours."

Am I wrong?

I am recalling my own first love: the cherished trinkets, the signed high-school graduation portrait, the mushy letters from army camp. We loved! Desperately we loved—in the chaste, honorable fashion of our generation.

True to the rules of our generation, we strangled our romance with our own timetable. Both of us had too much to accomplish separately before we were joined together in a way no man could put asunder.

I think with tenderness now of that innocent love. My reason is transparent, isn't it, Saviour? An unfulfilled romance is what my daughter needs at this stage in her life. Not marriage.

(Marriage jolts her timetable out of kilter.)

How can my daughter ponder the establishment of her *own* home when she refuses to lift a finger in mine? My Jesus, did I train her so poorly that she can invent one million excuses for failure to empty the dishwasher?

She is not without knowledge in the homemaking arts. During her high-school years she performed regular household chores—not eagerly, but at least resignedly. You can't fight City Hall—or Mother! Now, apparently, she can fight. She agrees—but fails to perform.

My husband advises, "Ask nothing. Leave her alone. Avoid controversy. Expect nothing from her. Then you won't be disappointed."

I feel intensely that this is wrong. I feel that she and I should be working together now—covering all areas from basic dusting to the philosophy of happy marriage. That she establishes herself as Queen Bee is an indication (to me) that she lacks maturity for the marriage relationship.

God, help us!

In front of me, Good Shepherd, is a list of expenses: invitations, flowers, wedding gown, bridesmaids' gifts, reception. . . . The total price—as estimated—is staggering.

Lord, forgive me for being resentful at the cost of this wedding I do not want. Money is only one measure of the cost. Physically and mentally, I am exhausted. It is my emotional attitude that drains my energy. I know that. But I cannot brainwash myself into a state of joy, feeling as I do that this match—at this time—will end in disaster.

God—help us.

43

Honored Father, the Generation Gap between humans extends its tentacles even to the ritual of marriage. My daughter and I lock horns in honest battle. I will not tolerate a lack of dignity during a church service. My daughter is equally determined to supplant parts of the traditional wedding rites with readings from popular literature. Lord, why must these youngsters assault everything my generation holds sacred?

Times do change. Humanity moves forward—but must it be at the cost of religious tradition?

So my daughter and I have left cautious courtesy behind. We battle openly. Lord, help me to erase this strain between us! Prohibit me from imposing my will merely because I control the checkbook.

Guide us. Help us to eliminate the tinsel from the warp and woof of Christian marriage. This wedding will be in Your house and to Your glory.

Bless it. Make it last.

We have compromised.

She, her fiance, and the minister will work out the details of the marriage ceremony. Her father and I, in return, are granted the right to select and word the invitations. It is a grudging compromise on her part.

Are you aware, Good Shepherd, that wedding invitations come in colors nowadays? That they might be embossed with decorations? Splashed with gold crosses? Worded in joyful, modern terms?

Gentle God, is it wrong for me to cling so desperately to tradition?

With Your guidance, I gain understanding of my own stubbornness. Somehow I equate the ancient rites and etiquette with traditional morality. Traditional morality is what I yearn to hand down to my daughter, and to her children, and to their children forever onward.

Stay with us and guide us, God—generation on end.

Holy Consoler, comfort me. I am deeply troubled by my daughter's poisonous tongue. She is snapping sharp criticisms that devastate me. Understand that I do not have a rhinoceros hide—we have always been a family protective of each other's feelings.

Is she merely pressured by the chores that precede a formal wedding? Irritated by too much mother-and-daughter togetherness? Or is the cause of her poison tongue more serious? Has she realized that this premature marriage is foolhardy?

If so, Supporting Friend, please guide her to the proper action. Convince her that it is not too late to back down. Convince her that marriage with doubts is the most foolish act of all.

I am Your agent; I shoulder this task as intermediary. But I am fearful. Please, God, let me deliver Your message free of Mother-knows-best pompousness.

For myself, I beg a rhinoceros-tough skin. I fear I am going to need it!

My daughter is suffering—anguished and shocked —because her best friend cannot serve as maid of honor. The circumstances that keep her away are not insurmountable from our view. Consequently the hurt etches deep.

God, ease my daughter's disappointment. Hold her steady in her loyalties.

Help her maintain this friendship despite the setback to it.

Creator, I am jealous and hurt. My daughter turns away from us and toward her prospective parents-in-law, spending much time with them—giving them the devotion she denies us.

Grant me the wisdom to rejoice that they enjoy each other's companionship. Remind me that she will return to us emotionally at a less traumatic time.

Restrain me from demanding her attentions now.

How glum and unloved I was feeling, Holy Spirit, when an holiday plant arrived—a poinsettia—flamboyant in size and color. Such a showy monster!

Sight of the florist's truck dismayed me. Was my mood so transparent that my husband noted it? I had tried hard to hide my inner turmoil from him. He had doubts enough to handle without being burdened by mine.

Surprise. The bouquet was not from my husband but from my daughter and her fiance. "Thank you for all you are doing," said the note.

My eyes misted. This was the first word of thanks I had received since the prewedding ordeal began. How the lack of gratitude had rankled me!

But my child is not ungrateful. She is not unfeeling. She is trapped by prewedding tensions—as I am.

God, help me to remove the barriers between us. Open our avenues of communication so her last weeks beneath this roof will be relaxed and pleasant.

Saviour, I feel such a failure as a mother! I yearn for closeness with my child and achieve instead an armed truce. How can I share her joy when I am saturated with terror?

God, help her to understand my love is worried but not cruel. Help me to show love that is not shadowed by my own broken dreams.

Help us!

Master, I am overwhelmed by the kindnesses of my friends. It is they who have switched these pre-wedding days from ordeal to delight. They support me. Their strength is mine.

Would You believe I am relaxed and having fun? My friends entertain with warmth and joy for the bride-elect. In response she sparkles. She is so much in love—she is a delight to watch.

My friends anticipate my needs. They offer housing for out-of-town guests. They volunteer food for the massing relatives. They suggest "baby-sitting" the wedding gifts during our absences from home, to stave off robberies.

Emotionally, too, they contribute—confiding all was not smooth as their own daughters neared marriage. This is important for me to hear. It eases the ache somewhat.

Thank You for these good friends, Lord!

Guardian of Mankind, here I sit at home, a nervous madonna, while my daughter pays her premarital visit to the doctor. There are facts she still needs to learn—information I find difficult to voice. I am snagged in the trap of my generation, recognizing the importance of sexual instruction yet finding the subject too personal to share even with my own daughter.

Of course we can discuss scientific, biological data. It is the union of man with woman—the pleasure of the act—the female technique—that builds a wall across our dialogue.

She reads books, and so do I. How frank these books are nowadays! I am grateful for them.

Today I pray, Lord, for our doctor's wisdom. Help him to ferret out the gaps in my child's knowledge.

Guide him in guiding her.

Kind God, each day there is less knotting in my stomach—less throbbing at my temples. Family tensions are easing. I am so grateful!

My daughter is less a porcupine and more a dove as a huge X on the wall calendar obliterates each finished day. Now we measure time in terms of the wedding date. If dates had shape and form, we could reach out and grasp this one.

Creator, the anniversary of Your birth approaches, as well. Save us from too much entanglement in our own affairs.

Always and forever, let us balance our lives to serve and worship You.

Generous God, please help my daughter to see beyond the dazzle of silver, the twinkle of crystal, the texture of towels. . . . Mentally she places each gift into use, shared by herself and her husband with the rest of the world shut out.

Lord, help her to see that every elegantly wrapped present represents thoughtful debate and, possibly, sacrifice on the part of the sender. Help her to understand that this deluge of household equipment is, indeed, a dowry of love.

How touching, truly: a dowry of love!

Charitable Saviour, we have just discovered that our prospective son-in-law has a cushion of savings. He and our daughter will not begin married life as freeloaders.

Oh, my jangled nerves! If only I had known this sooner!

Jesus, calm me. Guide me in separating that which is my business and that which is not.

Renew my trust that You will provide.

Our clan gathers from great distances, as it traditionally does in time of joy or sorrow. King of Glory, thank You for the supporting love of our families!

God, my Father, my devotion knows no limit. Thank You! Thank You! Because of Your constant presence, I have survived these months of worry and uncertainty and turmoil. If I managed competently, it is because I lean so heavily on You.

All is in readiness. The rehearsal went well, each participant serious in his duties.

Tomorrow night, the wedding. . . .

Remain with us, Lord of Lords.

The morning is laced with sunlight. In twelve hours my daughter will trade marriage vows with a young man personable but unemployed.

Let me forget this major worry today, King of Heaven. Prompt me with words to express my love and devotion to my child. If only she might believe how sincere are my wishes for her lasting happiness!

Guide my tongue, oh, God, so I say only that which is pertinent. Allow me to utter no word of advice.

The time for advice is past. That deadline was reached.

Fortunately there is no deadline on prayer. Help me, Lord.

I cry.

The bride is dazzling, her joy is like a torch. On the trembling arm of her father, she moves toward her handsome bridegroom with such confidence— I suddenly share her faith. Although their future is uncertain, it will be good. Together they will build.

God, be with them!

Sweet Saviour, even religion has its frontiers. The solemn, patterned, traditional wedding ceremony is in a state of flux. Participants now are free to inject readings that are meaningful to them personally. (Oh, God, that word *meaningful* again! How it grates against my conventional, conservative mores.)

Yet on this occasion, I am deeply stirred by the personalized supplements. This ceremony—different from all others—reflects the sentimental and optimistic character of my daughter.

Such a frontier in religion is good, I decide. Perhaps there is danger of our worshiping by rote. Here, instead, is a young couple who have written a part of themselves into an ancient sacrament. So doing, they underline partnership with God and the permanency of their vows.

Saviour, how wise You are!

Master, the solemnity of these rites helps me to recognize my child in her new role—that of wife. For Your sacraments which bring peace and direction to our lives, I thank You.

Amid the reception hubbub, my daughter managed to speak private words with me, and I with her. In our new roles we will build a close relationship, I think. Be with us, God, as we strive to forget old irritations while remembering pleasures. Guide us to new respect and understanding.

Their honeymoon destination is undisclosed. How in character! The route for their lives—immediate and long-range—also is undisclosed.

For the remarkable fact that I no longer worry, I thank You, God. Oh, it is not true that I do not worry! After all, I am a mother. I shall always want the best for my child.

What has been lifted from my shoulders is the weighty burden of despair—the terror that this is a mismatch—the doubt they can financially survive.

I have achieved this peace of mind through faith in a Supreme Being and also—surprisingly— through faith in this young, fearless, and astonishing generation we somehow have produced.

Thank You, Lord!

How enduring is the love I feel for my husband, and he for me. Tonight begins a new segment in our good life together. No longer are we primarily parents—we are free now to be lovers. Already I taste delight in this new freedom.

If it is Your will, God, please grant us long life together.